BIBLE STUDIES

Ignite Your Passion for God

Kay Arthur & Mark Sheldrake

PRECEPT MINISTRIES INTERNATIONAL

WATERBROOK
PRESS

CONTENTS

HOW TO USE THIS STUDY

This small-group study is for people who are interested in learning for themselves more about what the Bible says on various subjects, but who have only limited time to meet together. It's ideal, for example, for a lunch group at work, an early morning men's group, a young mothers' group meeting in a home, a Sunday-school class, or even family devotions. (It's also ideal for small groups that typically have longer meeting times—such as evening groups or Saturday morning groups—but want to devote only a portion of their time together to actual study, while reserving the rest for prayer, fellowship, or other activities.)

This book is designed so that all the group's participants will complete each lesson's study activities *at the same time*. Discussing your insights drawn from what God says about the subject reveals exciting, life-impacting truths.

Although it's a group study, you'll need a facilitator to lead the study and keep the discussion moving. If *you* are your group's facilitator, the leader, here are some helpful points for making your job easier:

- Go through the lesson and mark the text before you lead the group. This will give you increased familiarity with the material and will enable you to facilitate the group with greater ease. It may be easier for you to lead the group through the instructions for marking if you, as a leader, choose a specific color for each symbol you mark.

- As you lead the group, start at the beginning of the text and simply read it aloud in the order it appears in the lesson, including the Insight boxes, which appear throughout. Work through the lesson together, observing and discussing what you learn. As you read the Scripture verses, have the group say aloud the word they are marking in the text.

- The discussion questions are there simply to help you cover the material. As the class moves into the discussion, many times you will find that they will cover the questions on their own. Remember, the discussion questions are there to guide the group through the topic, not to squelch discussion.

- Remember how important it is for people to verbalize their answers and discoveries. This greatly strengthens their personal understanding of each week's lesson. Try to ensure that everyone has plenty of opportunity to contribute to each week's discussions.

- Keep the discussion moving. This may mean spending more time on some parts of the study than on others. If necessary, you should feel free to spread out a lesson over more than one session. However, remember that you don't want to slow the pace too much. It's much better to leave everyone wanting more than to have people dropping out because of declining interest.

- If the validity or accuracy of some of the answers seems questionable, you can gently and cheerfully remind the group to stay focused on the truth of the Scriptures. Your object is to learn what the Bible says, not to engage in human philosophy. Simply stick with the Scriptures and give God the opportunity to speak. His Word *is* truth (John 17:17)!

IGNITE YOUR PASSION FOR GOD

Have you ever jumped in the car, started it, and then found yourself at your destination with no clear idea of how you got there?

It's a weird feeling to realize you are awake but mentally you have checked out. What's even worse is when operating on autopilot places you on a road you never intended, such as when you realize you're driving to work when you planned to go to the grocery store.

A similar situation can occur in our spiritual lives when we operate on autopilot, doing things out of habit rather than out of a burning passion to serve God.

Sadly, so many of us find at different times in our spiritual journey that we've developed apathy toward the things of God. The dictionary describes *apathy* as "the absence or suppression of passion, emotion, or excitement."

It's a dullness of heart that affects the way you look

at life. In the life of a believer, spiritual apathy might appear as a subtly decreasing interest in God and the things of God. A dullness of hearing when it comes to reading the Word of God and to hearing about the work of God. It's a lethargy, a sluggish feeling toward anything Christian.

Do you find yourself…

- reluctant to gather with other believers?
- finding multiple reasons to miss church, Bible study, and prayer meetings?
- singing the hymns and choruses rotely, as empty words on the screen or in a book?
- constantly looking to the negative aspects of church and grumbling about them?
- turning not to the Bible but to the latest quick-fix spiritual growth book?

Does this describe your life? Are you noticing others around you who are on fire for Jesus? And do you wonder how you can ignite a fire that will propel you toward a deeper, more meaningful understanding of God?

Over the next six lessons we will explore why and how we become apathetic to the things of God. Our prayer is that through these lessons you will open your heart and mind to the truths of God and let them ignite a passion and fire that cannot be extinguished.

Perhaps you've never truly known a burning passion for spiritual things. Or maybe your love for Jesus once burned brightly and He was your highest priority in life, but now the coals are barely glowing and your heart seems to be growing colder.

What is it that prevents you from experiencing an excitement for the things of God?

This week we will look at Scripture passages that give us insight into some things that smother our spiritual fires.

OBSERVE

Old and advanced in years, King David chose his son Solomon to be the next king of Israel. As David neared death, he charged Solomon to "Be strong…show yourself a man" (1 Kings 2:2). He urged his son to walk in God's ways and "keep His statutes, His commandments, His ordinances, and His testimonies, according to what is written in the Law of Moses" (2:3). Soon after this, David died and, as 1 Kings 2:46 tells us, "Thus the kingdom was established in the hands of Solomon."

Let's see what happened next and what we can learn for our lives.

Leader: Read 1 Kings 3:1–9 aloud. Have the group say aloud and…
- *mark with a downward semicircle, like this ⌒, every reference to Solomon, including pronouns and synonyms.*

1 KINGS 3:1–9

1 Then Solomon formed a marriage alliance with Pharaoh king of Egypt, and took Pharaoh's daughter and brought her to

the city of David until he had finished building his own house and the house of the LORD and the wall around Jerusalem.

2 The people were still sacrificing on the high places, because there was no house built for the name of the LORD until those days.

3 Now Solomon loved the LORD, walking in the statutes of his father David, except he sacrificed and burned incense on the high places.

4 The king went to Gibeon to sacrifice there, for that was the great high place; Solomon offered a thousand burnt offerings on that altar.

• *mark every reference to **the Lord**, including pronouns such as **You** and synonyms such as **God**, with a triangle:*

△

• *underline the word **discern**.*

As you read the text, it's helpful to have the group say the key words aloud as they mark them. This way everyone will be sure they are marking every occurrence of the word, including any synonymous words or phrases. Do this throughout the study.

DISCUSS

• How is Solomon described in these verses?

• What does verse 3 reveal about Solomon's behavior as king?

• What does this tell you about Solomon's heart toward God?

5 In Gibeon the LORD appeared to Solomon in a dream at night; and God said, "Ask what you wish Me to give you."

6 Then Solomon said, "You have shown great lovingkindness to Your servant David my father, according as he walked before You in truth and righteousness and uprightness of heart toward You; and You have reserved for him this great lovingkindness, that You have given him a son to sit on his throne, as it is this day.

7 "Now, O LORD my God, You have made Your servant king in place of my

father David, yet I am but a little child; I do not know how to go out or come in.

8 "Your servant is in the midst of Your people which You have chosen, a great people who are too many to be numbered or counted.

9 "So give Your servant an understanding heart to judge Your people to discern between good and evil. For who is able to judge this great people of Yours?"

• What did Solomon request of God?

• What is the significance of his request in light of verse 7?

1 KINGS 3:10–15

10 It was pleasing in the sight of the Lord that Solomon had asked this thing.

OBSERVE

Solomon had put his request before the Lord: he wanted a discerning heart to know the difference between good and evil so he could lead God's people. How did God respond to this request?

Leader: Read 1 Kings 3:10–15 aloud and have the group…

- *mark every reference to* **Solomon,** *including pronouns, with a semi-circle:* /‾\

- *draw a triangle over every reference to* **the Lord,** *including* **You** *and* **God:** △

- *underline the words* **discernment** *and* **discerning.**

DISCUSS

- What was God's response to Solomon's request? What reason did God give?

11 God said to him, "Because you have asked this thing and have not asked for yourself long life, nor have asked riches for yourself, nor have you asked for the life of your enemies, but have asked for yourself discernment to understand justice,

12 behold, I have done according to your words. Behold, I have given you a wise and discerning heart, so that there has been no one like you before you, nor shall one like you arise after you.

13 "I have also given you what you have not asked, both riches and honor, so that there will not be any among

the kings like you all your days.

14 "If you walk in My ways, keeping My statutes and commandments, as your father David walked, then I will prolong your days."

15 Then Solomon awoke, and behold, it was a dream. And he came to Jerusalem and stood before the ark of the covenant of the Lord, and offered burnt offerings and made peace offerings, and made a feast for all his servants.

1 KINGS 11:1–11

1 Now King Solomon loved many foreign women...

2 from the nations concerning which the

• When Solomon made his request before God, who or what was Solomon's greatest concern? Look back at verse 8 on page 6. Don't miss a detail in respect to the people.

• What insight does this give you into Solomon's heart, his passion for God?

OBSERVE

God answered Solomon's prayer. He gave him "wisdom and very great discernment and breadth of mind" (1 Kings 4:29) so that people came from all over to hear his wisdom. The next few chapters of 1 Kings detail how Solomon built the house of the

Lord, and the Lord's glory and presence filled it. He then spent thirteen years building his own house. King Solomon became greater than all the kings of the earth in riches and in wisdom (1 Kings 10:23). Then we come to 1 Kings 11.

Leader: Read 1 Kings 11:1–11 and have the group…

- *mark the references to **Solomon** as before.*
- *draw a heart over every reference to **the heart**, like this:*♡
- *mark the references to **the Lord** with a triangle.*

DISCUSS

- What do you learn from marking the references to Solomon's heart? Don't miss a detail!

LORD had said to the sons of Israel, "You shall not associate with them, nor shall they associate with you, for they will surely turn your heart away after their gods." Solomon held fast to these in love.

³ He had seven hundred wives, princesses, and three hundred concubines, and his wives turned his heart away.

⁴ For when Solomon was old, his wives turned his heart away after other gods; and his heart was not wholly devoted to the LORD his God, as the heart of David his father had been.

⁵ For Solomon went after Ashtoreth the

goddess of the Sidonians and after Milcom the detestable idol of the Ammonites.

6 Solomon did what was evil in the sight of the LORD, and did not follow the LORD fully, as David his father had done.

7 Then Solomon built a high place for Chemosh the detestable idol of Moab, on the mountain which is east of Jerusalem, and for Molech the detestable idol of the sons of Ammon.

8 Thus also he did for all his foreign wives, who burned incense and sacrificed to their gods.

• According to verse 6, where did Solomon fail?

• What happened as a result?

• What does the text tell you about the Lord's feeling and response to Solomon?

• What in your life has the potential to draw your heart away from the Lord?

⁹ Now the LORD was angry with Solomon because his heart was turned away from the LORD, the God of Israel, who had appeared to him twice,

¹⁰ and had commanded him concerning this thing, that he should not go after other gods; but he did not observe what the LORD had commanded.

¹¹ So the LORD said to Solomon, "Because you have done this, and you have not kept My covenant and My statutes, which I have commanded you, I will surely tear the kingdom from you, and will give it to your servant."

EXODUS 20:1–6

¹ Then God spoke all these words, saying,

² "I am the LORD your God, who brought you out of the land of Egypt, out of the house of slavery.

³ "You shall have no other gods before Me.

⁴ "You shall not make for yourself an idol, or any likeness of what is in heaven above or on the earth beneath or in the water under the earth.

⁵ "You shall not worship them or serve them; for I, the LORD your God, am a jealous God, visiting the iniquity of the fathers

OBSERVE

Leader: Read Exodus 20:1–6 and have the group...

- *mark all references to **the Lord**, including pronouns, with a triangle.*
- *mark **gods** and **idols**, including synonyms and pronouns, with a big **I**.*
- *draw a heart over the word **love**.*

DISCUSS

• What did you learn about God?

• List what you learned from marking the references to idols.

• If an idol is anything that moves God out of His rightful place, anything that you bow down to, give greater worth than you give to God, what would be some common idols in your culture? Among your peers?

INSIGHT

Idol worship does not necessarily mean we have a golden calf or wooden image on our mantle that we bow to three times a day. An idol can be anything we put above our relationship with God, or whatever steals our heart away from God. It can be money, power, relationships—anything we treasure above God. In Colossians 3:5 we read that greed is a form of idolatry.

on the children, on the third and the fourth generations of those who hate Me,

6 but showing lovingkindness to thousands, to those who love Me and keep My commandments.

• From what you've observed in your life and in others, in what ways do idols draw us away from God? Seek to smother our passion for God?

• Is anything in your life taking priority over God? Would you consider it an idol? Why or why not?

DEUTERONOMY 30:15–20

15 See, I have set before you today life and prosperity, and death and adversity;

16 in that I command you today to love the LORD your God, to walk in His ways and to keep His commandments and His statutes and His judgments, that you may live and multiply, and that the LORD your God may bless you in the land where you are entering to possess it.

17 But if your heart turns away and you will not obey, but are drawn away and worship other gods and serve them,

18 I declare to you today that you shall

OBSERVE

God is clear about His expectations for those who claim to follow Him. Let's look at what God, through Moses, told His people, Israel, just before He took them into the Promised Land.

Leader: Read Deuteronomy 30:15–20. Have the group...
- *draw a triangle over every reference to* **the Lord,** *including pronouns.*
- *underline every reference to **the Israelites,** including **you** and **your.***
- *mark **heart** and **love** with a heart.*

INSIGHT

Deuteronomy is the fifth book of the Law, also known as the Torah. The idea behind the word *Torah* is "to inform, instruct, and guide."

DISCUSS

- What did you learn from marking the references to God? What choice was He offering?

- Moses gave three clear instructions for how God's people should live. What are they? (Hint: look at verse 16.) Number the instructions as you find them in the text.

- What evidence of spiritual passion do you find in these verses? What precedes obeying God and holding fast to Him?

- In Scripture the word *but* indicates a contrast. What contrast is made in this passage?

- So we don't miss it, what did Moses say would draw God's people away from Him?

- What are the consequences of our heart turning away from God? What does it look like when we turn toward Him?

- What do verses 19–20 say regarding those who choose to obey?

surely perish. You will not prolong your days in the land where you are crossing the Jordan to enter and possess it.

19 I call heaven and earth to witness against you today, that I have set before you life and death, the blessing and the curse. So choose life in order that you may live, you and your descendants,

20 by loving the LORD your God, by obeying His voice, and by holding fast to Him; for this is your life and the length of your days, that you may live in the land which the LORD swore to your fathers, to Abraham, Isaac, and Jacob, to give them.

MARK 12:28–34

28 One of the scribes came and heard them arguing, and recognizing that He had answered them well, asked Him, "What commandment is the foremost of all?"

29 Jesus answered, "The foremost is, 'Hear, O Israel! The LORD our God is one LORD;

30 And you shall love the LORD your God with all your heart, and with all your soul, and with all your mind, and with all your strength.'

31 "The second is this, 'You shall love your neighbor as yourself.' There is no other

OBSERVE

Let's jump ahead to the New Testament, where Jesus referred to the Deuteronomy 30 passage to answer a question from a scribe, who was an expert in the Law.

Leader: Read Mark 12:28–34 and have the group...

- *underline **Israel** and the pronouns **you** and **your** in reference to the people.*
- *draw a heart over the word **love.***

DISCUSS

- What did Jesus say was the foremost commandment? Underline it.

- What was the second commandment? Underline it.

- What did you learn about love in this passage?

- What helpful descriptions, if any, do you find regarding what it looks like to have passion for God?

- Just so you don't miss it, to what degree are we to love God?

- How would following these commandments shape our daily choices?

commandment greater than these."

³² The scribe said to Him, "Right, Teacher; You have truly stated that He is One, and there is no one else besides Him;

³³ and to love Him with all the heart and with all the under-standing and with all the strength, and to love one's neighbor as himself, is much more than all burnt offerings and sacrifices."

³⁴ When Jesus saw that he had answered intelligently, He said to him, "You are not far from the kingdom of God." After that, no one would venture to ask Him any more questions.

WRAP IT UP

We saw in our study this week how our hearts can be drawn away from loving God when we allow anything or anyone to take precedence over Him.

In Matthew 6:21, Jesus taught that where our treasure lies, our hearts will follow. Though Solomon initially found his treasure in the Lord, it seems as he grew older, he found his treasure in his wives and was therefore drawn to false gods.

Like Solomon, so many believers have left their first love and don't know it. They've given a portion of their hearts over to their own desires and the things of this world, mistakenly believing they can serve both.

Are you trying to make room in your heart for both the kingdom of God and the treasures of this world? It will never work out. God tells us He is a jealous God. He must be first. You can't be consumed with love and passion for Jesus Christ if you have a divided heart.

The first step in moving forward is to confess to God that you have left your first love. Repent—have a change of mind, of heart. Tell God you want to love Him with all your heart, soul, mind, and strength. Ask Him to remove the idols that have crowded into your life and to kindle the fire of passion in your heart.

When you are sitting beside a campfire and notice the flame dying down, most likely you'll start looking for a good dry piece of wood to throw on the fire as fuel. What does a Christian do when the flame of their passion for the Lord dwindles? This week we will look at how God's Word serves as spiritual fuel—and what happens to our passion when we fail to spend time in the Bible.

OBSERVE

In Deuteronomy 17:14–20 Moses prophesied that Israel would request a king, and he gave specific directives for their future ruler. As we look at these directives, pay careful attention to Moses' instructions concerning the Law.

Leader: *Read Deuteronomy 17:14–20. Have the group say aloud and...*

- *mark all references to **the king**, including synonyms such as **one** and pronouns such as **he** and **himself**, with a semicircle:* ⌒
- *draw a heart over the word **heart**, like this:* ♡
- *mark all references to **the Law**, including **commandment**, with an open book, like this:* 📖

DEUTERONOMY 17:14–20

14 When you enter the land which the LORD your God gives you, and you possess it and live in it, and you say, "I will set a king over me like all the nations who are around me,"

15 you shall surely set a king over you whom the LORD your God

chooses, one from among your countrymen you shall set as king over yourselves; you may not put a foreigner over yourselves who is not your countryman.

16 Moreover, he shall not multiply horses for himself, nor shall he cause the people to return to Egypt to multiply horses, since the LORD has said to you, "You shall never again return that way."

17 He shall not multiply wives for himself, or else his heart will turn away; nor shall he greatly increase silver and gold for himself.

18 Now it shall come about when he sits on

DISCUSS

• What did you learn from marking the references to the king?

• Who would select the king who was to rule?

• What was the king's responsibility in relationship to the Law?

• How does what you have learned about the Law and the king apply to your life today?

• Now discuss what you learn from marking *heart*, keeping in mind what you learned last week. How can this be applied to your life?

the throne of his kingdom, he shall write for himself a copy of this law on a scroll in the presence of the Levitical priests.

19 It shall be with him and he shall read it all the days of his life, that he may learn to fear the LORD his God, by carefully observing all the words of this law and these statutes,

20 that his heart may not be lifted up above his countrymen and that he may not turn aside from the commandment, to the right or the left, so that he and his sons may continue long in his kingdom in the midst of Israel.

2 CHRONICLES 34:1–7

¹ Josiah was eight years old when he became king, and he reigned thirty-one years in Jerusalem.

² He did right in the sight of the LORD, and walked in the ways of his father David and did not turn aside to the right or to the left.

³ For in the eighth year of his reign while he was still a youth, he began to seek the God of his father David; and in the twelfth year he began to purge Judah and Jerusalem of the high places, the Asherim, the carved images and the molten images.

⁴ They tore down the altars of the Baals in his

OBSERVE

In 931 BC, because Solomon did not follow the Lord fully but did evil in the sight of the Lord, Israel split into two kingdoms, the north being Israel and the south being Judah. The southern kingdom, Judah, was witness to a number of kings who did not follow in the footsteps of David. Two of the worst, Manasseh and Amon, promoted idol worship among the people of Judah. We pick up the story after the reign of these evil rulers, about 640 BC. There's a new king in town, and his name is Josiah. He is the son of Amon and the grandson of Manasseh. Does he even stand a chance of being a man of God, given his heritage?

Leader: *Read 2 Chronicles 34:1–7 aloud. Have the group say aloud and…*

- *draw a semicircle over each reference to* **Josiah,** *just as you did for* **the king.**
- *circle any references to* **time.**
- *mark with a big* **I** *each reference to* **idols,** *including pronouns and synonyms such as* **images, Baals, Asherim, altar.**

DISCUSS

• What do you learn about Josiah in verses 1–2?

• In verse 3 what are we told about the king's actions at different points early in his reign? Based on verse 1, how old was he when he took these actions? And what does that suggest about Josiah's heart?

• What insight do Josiah's actions in the twelfth year of his reign (verses 4–7) give us into the state of affairs in Judah at this time?

presence, and the incense altars that were high above them he chopped down; also the Asherim, the carved images and the molten images he broke in pieces and ground to powder and scattered it on the graves of those who had sacrificed to them.

5 Then he burned the bones of the priests on their altars and purged Judah and Jerusalem.

6 In the cities of Manasseh, Ephraim, Simeon, even as far as Naphtali, in their surrounding ruins,

7 he also tore down the altars and beat the Asherim and the carved images into powder, and chopped

down all the incense altars throughout the land of Israel. Then he returned to Jerusalem.

2 CHRONICLES 34:8–10, 14–21

8 Now in the eighteenth year of his reign, when he had purged the land and the house, he sent Shaphan the son of Azaliah, and Maaseiah an official of the city, and Joah the son of Joahaz the recorder, to repair the house of the LORD his God.

9 They came to Hilkiah the high priest and delivered the money that was brought into the house of God, which the Levites, the doorkeepers, had collected from Manasseh and Ephraim, and from

• What parallels, if any, do you see in your nation?

OBSERVE

According to 2 Chronicles 34:3, in the twelfth year of his reign Josiah was twenty years old when he purged the land of idols. Let's see what Josiah did next.

Leader: Read 2 Chronicles 34:8–10, 14–21 aloud. Have the group do the following:
- *Mark every mention of **Josiah**, including pronouns, and **the king**, with a semicircle.*
- *Draw a box around **house of the Lord:** [   ]*
- *Mark the phrases **book of the law** and **words of the law** with an open book, like this: ⟁⟁*

DISCUSS

• According to verse 8, how old was Josiah at this point, and what had he accomplished by this time?

INSIGHT

The idols date back to the time of Manasseh's reign. The grandfather of Josiah was a man who "seduced" the people of Judah "to do evil more than the nations whom the LORD destroyed before the sons of Israel (2 Kings 21:9).

When Manasseh died, his son Amon (Josiah's father) became king at age twenty-two. He reigned two years and "did evil in the sight of the LORD, as Manasseh his father had done" (2 Kings 21:20).

Amon was killed by his servants, and at age eight Josiah inherited this godless nation.

---

all the remnant of Israel, and from all Judah and Benjamin and the inhabitants of Jerusalem.

10 Then they gave it into the hands of the workmen who had the oversight of the house of the LORD, and the workmen who were working in the house of the LORD used it to restore and repair the house....

14 When they were bringing out the money which had been brought into the house of the LORD, Hilkiah the priest found the book of the law of the LORD given by Moses.

15 Hilkiah responded and said to Shaphan the scribe, "I have found the book of the law in the

house of the LORD."
And Hilkiah gave the
book to Shaphan.

16 Then Shaphan
brought the book to
the king and reported
further word to the
king, saying, "Every-
thing that was
entrusted to your ser-
vants they are doing.

17 "They have also
emptied out the money
which was found in the
house of the LORD, and
have delivered it into the
hands of the supervisors
and the workmen."

18 Moreover, Shaphan
the scribe told the king
saying, "Hilkiah the
priest gave me a book."
And Shaphan read
from it in the presence
of the king.

• What was next on Josiah's agenda? What
insight does this give you into the heart of
this king?

• When the house of the Lord was being
repaired, what was found? Where?

• What does this tell you? What parallels
do you see regarding the church today?

• What was Josiah's reaction to hearing the
words of the Law? Why did he react this
way?

INSIGHT

Deuteronomy 17:18 declared that when a king took the throne, he was to write out the book of the Law in the presence of the Levitical priests. Hezekiah, who reigned from 730–686 BC, was the last king who did right in the sight of the Lord in Judah. Following him were Manasseh and Amon, both doing evil and not following the book of the Law. The people of Judah had been without the Law for fifty-seven years.

• How would you describe the significance of the discovery made in the temple? Explain your answer.

19 When the king heard the words of the law, he tore his clothes.

20 Then the king commanded Hilkiah, Ahikam the son of Shaphan, Abdon the son of Micah, Shaphan the scribe, and Asaiah the king's servant, saying,

21 "Go, inquire of the LORD for me and for those who are left in Israel and in Judah, concerning the words of the book which has been found; for great is the wrath of the LORD which is poured out on us because our fathers have not observed the word of the LORD, to do according to all that is written in this book."

2 CHRONICLES 34:22–28

22 So Hilkiah and those whom the king had told went to Huldah the prophetess, the wife of Shallum the son of Tokhath, the son of Hasrah, the keeper of the wardrobe (now she lived in Jerusalem in the Second Quarter); and they spoke to her regarding this.

23 She said to them, "Thus says the LORD, the God of Israel, 'Tell the man who sent you to Me,

24 thus says the LORD, "Behold, I am bringing evil on this place and on its inhabitants, even all the curses written in the book which they have

OBSERVE

After years of idolatry throughout Judah, the book of the Law had been found, and Josiah learned that the nation was about to experience God's wrath as a result of their disobedience. He understandably had some questions for the Lord, as we saw in 2 Chronicles 34:21. Let's continue in our study and find out what happened next.

Leader: Read 2 Chronicles 34:22–28. Have the group do the following:

- *Mark with a semicircle the words **king, man, you,** and **him** as they refer to **Josiah**.*
- *Draw a triangle over every reference to **the Lord,** including pronouns.*
- *Mark **heart** with a heart.*
- *Draw an open book over the references to **the Law,** such as **book** and **words.***

DISCUSS

• According to verses 24–25, what message did God send to Josiah? What was God going to do and why?

• In what ways, if any, do you think God's people today have provoked His judgment? Explain your answer.

• Look at where you marked the references to the king. How did Josiah humble himself?

read in the presence of the king of Judah.

25 "Because they have forsaken Me and have burned incense to other gods, that they might provoke Me to anger with all the works of their hands; therefore My wrath will be poured out on this place and it shall not be quenched."'

26 "But to the king of Judah who sent you to inquire of the LORD, thus you will say to him, 'Thus says the LORD God of Israel regarding the words which you have heard,

27 "Because your heart was tender and you humbled yourself before God when you

heard His words against this place and against its inhabitants, and because you humbled yourself before Me, tore your clothes and wept before Me, I truly have heard you," declares the LORD.

28 "Behold, I will gather you to your fathers and you shall be gathered to your grave in peace, so your eyes will not see all the evil which I will bring on this place and on its inhabitants." ' " And they brought back word to the king.

• What was the result of Josiah's tender heart and humility?

• What lessons, if any, do you see for us today? Discuss.

OBSERVE

God promised to hold back His wrath on Judah as long as Josiah was alive. Let's look at Josiah's response to this news.

Leader: Read 2 Chronicles 34:29–33. Have the group say aloud and...
- *mark **Josiah** with a semicircle.*
- *draw a book over all references to **God's Word**, including **book of the covenant, commandments, testimonies,** and so on.*
- *mark **heart** with a heart.*

DISCUSS

- Who was with Josiah, and where did they go?

- What did Josiah do in the house of the Lord?

2 CHRONICLES 34:29–33

29 Then the king sent and gathered all the elders of Judah and Jerusalem.

30 The king went up to the house of the LORD and all the men of Judah, the inhabitants of Jerusalem, the priests, the Levites and all the people, from the greatest to the least; and he read in their hearing all the words of the book of the covenant which was found in the house of the LORD.

31 Then the king stood in his place and made a covenant before the LORD to walk after the LORD, and to keep His commandments and His

testimonies and His statutes with all his heart and with all his soul, to perform the words of the covenant written in this book.

32 Moreover, he made all who were present in Jerusalem and Benjamin to stand with him. So the inhabitants of Jerusalem did according to the covenant of God, the God of their fathers.

33 Josiah removed all the abominations from all the lands belonging to the sons of Israel, and made all who were present in Israel to serve the LORD their God. Throughout his lifetime they did not turn from following the LORD God of their fathers.

• A covenant is a solemn binding agreement. Who agreed to the covenant described in verse 31? What was the result of the covenant that was made that day?

• How do Josiah's actions relate to Deuteronomy 17:18–20, which we read at the beginning of this lesson?

OBSERVE

In 2 Chronicles 34:3–4 Josiah took two important actions. The first was to *seek the God of his father David even while "a youth."* He was sixteen! Second, he began to *purge* the land of the high places where Israel was worshiping false gods. In 2 Kings 23 we find a parallel passage that gives us a closer look at Josiah's actions as he purged the land.

Leader: Read 2 Kings 23:4–8, 10–11, 13, 19–20. Have the group say aloud and...

* *mark all references to **Josiah**, including pronouns, with a semicircle.*
* *circle all of **the things and people Josiah purged** from the land, such as **vessels, Asherah**, and so on.*

DISCUSS

* Move through the text and discuss everything you circled. Note where these things were and what insight this gives you into the state of the nation and the culture of Josiah's time.

---

2 KINGS 23:4–8, 10–11, 13, 19–20

4 Then the king commanded Hilkiah the high priest and the priests of the second order and the door-keepers, to bring out of the temple of the LORD all the vessels that were made for Baal, for Asherah, and for all the host of heaven; and he burned them outside Jerusalem in the fields of the Kidron, and carried their ashes to Bethel.

5 He did away with the idolatrous priests whom the kings of Judah had appointed to burn incense in the high places in the cities of Judah and in the surrounding area

of Jerusalem, also those who burned incense to Baal, to the sun and to the moon and to the constellations and to all the host of heaven.

6 He brought out the Asherah from the house of the LORD outside Jerusalem to the brook Kidron, and burned it at the brook Kidron, and ground it to dust, and threw its dust on the graves of the common people.

7 He also broke down the houses of the male cult prostitutes which were in the house of the LORD, where the women were weaving hangings for the Asherah.

• Do you see any parallels in your culture today? If so, how does this make you feel? Does it make you want to take any specific actions? What and why?

• Why wasn't it enough to seek the Lord? Why was it necessary to purge?

• Looking to Josiah's example, can you identify any things, activities, or people you need to purge from your life because they're taking priority that rightfully belongs to God?

• Now stop and think about what you've observed. What brought all this purging about?

8 Then he brought all the priests from the cities of Judah, and defiled the high places where the priests had burned incense, from Geba to Beersheba; and he broke down the high places of the gates which were at the entrance of the gate of Joshua the governor of the city, which were on one's left at the city gate....

10 He also defiled Topheth, which is in the valley of the son of Hinnom, that no man might make his son or his daughter pass through the fire for Molech.

11 He did away with the horses which the kings of Judah had given to the sun, at the entrance of the house of the LORD, by the chamber of Nathan-melech the official, which was in the precincts; and he burned the chariots of the sun with fire....

13 The high places which were before Jerusalem, which were on the right of the mount of destruction which Solomon the king of Israel had built for Ashtoreth the abomination of the Sidonians, and for Chemosh the abomination of Moab, and for Milcom the abomination of the sons of Ammon, the king defiled....

• What does this tell you about the role of the Word of God?

• As you study these passages this week, is there anything that makes you wonder if the Word of God has been lost in the house of God?

19 Josiah also removed all the houses of the high places which were in the cities of Samaria, which the kings of Israel had made provoking the LORD; and he did to them just as he had done in Bethel.

20 All the priests of the high places who were there he slaughtered on the altars and burned human bones on them; then he returned to Jerusalem.

2 KINGS 23:21–23

21 Then the king commanded all the people saying, "Celebrate the Passover to the LORD your God as it is written in this book of the covenant."

22 Surely such a Passover had not been celebrated from the days of the judges who judged Israel, nor in all the days of the kings of Israel and of the kings of Judah.

23 But in the eighteenth year of King Josiah, this Passover was observed to the LORD in Jerusalem.

OBSERVE

Leader: *Read 2 Kings 23:21–23 and have the group say aloud and mark…*

- *all references to* **Josiah,** *including pronouns, with a semicircle.*
- *every reference to* **the Passover** *with a big* **P.**

INSIGHT

God commanded His people to celebrate three feasts annually. The first of these was the Feast of Passover, which included the Feast of Unleavened Bread and the Feast of Firstfruits.

Passover was in commemoration of God's preservation of His people from the angel of death and their deliverance from their slavery in Egypt. It was to be celebrated every year on the fourteenth day of the first month (Leviticus 23:5).

DISCUSS

• What do you learn from marking the references to the Passover?

• Why was it to be celebrated?

• What does this tell you about Josiah's heart toward God in commanding the people to celebrate this feast?

• What role would the Word of God play in the life of someone who was passionate about God? What role does it play in your life today?

WRAP IT UP

Life is busy. Work is demanding. The things of this world are appealing, seductive! We go to bed exhausted. We wake up tired. And we live in a world of people who, for the most part, have no interest in the things of God. They don't keep His Word; in fact Jesus says they hate Him (John 15:18–25). This is the world we live in, a world that inevitably will smother our spiritual passion unless we continually fuel it with the living and active Word of God.

Jesus said that we live by every word that comes from the mouth of God (Matthew 4:4). God says, "Blessed are those who hunger and thirst for righteousness, for they shall be satisfied" (Matthew 5:6).

If we are true Christians, the genuine thing and not a hypocrite, then our bodies are His temple, the house of God. So the question is, what role does the Word of God have in your life? Has it gotten lost in His house?

In 2 Timothy 3:16–17 Paul wrote, "All Scripture is inspired by God and profitable for teaching, for reproof, for correction, for training in righteousness; so that the man of God may be adequate, equipped for every good work."

If we're going to love God with all our heart, soul, mind, and strength, we can't afford to neglect the inspired Word of God.

Christianity is a relationship with God. He speaks to us in His Word, and like the disciples of old, our hearts burn as He speaks and explains the Scriptures to us (Luke 24:32).

We speak to Him in prayer, and when we have truly communed with Him—when we know He has heard or spoken—a fire is kindled.

Through prayer, a fresh breath of the Spirit stirs the smoldering embers of love, causing them to burn brighter. Passion is stirred and hope flickers.

Our God is there! He hears! He's real—and we want more of Him!

OBSERVE

There is nothing like answered prayer to ignite our passion for God. And for us, at this point in our study, there is no better illustration than what happened to Manasseh, the evil grandfather of Josiah mentioned in our study last week.

Leader: Read 2 Chronicles 33:9–13 aloud. Have the group say aloud and…

- *underline every reference to **Manasseh**, including the pronouns **him, he, himself** when they refer to the king.*
- *put a triangle over every reference to **the Lord**, including pronouns.*
- *mark every reference to **entreating God, prayer, supplication** like this:*

2 CHRONICLES 33:9–13

9 Thus Manasseh misled Judah and the inhabitants of Jerusalem to do more evil than the nations whom the LORD destroyed before the sons of Israel.

10 The LORD spoke to Manasseh and his

people, but they paid no attention.

11 Therefore the LORD brought the commanders of the army of the king of Assyria against them, and they captured Manasseh with hooks, bound him with bronze chains and took him to Babylon.

12 When he was in distress, he entreated the LORD his God and humbled himself greatly before the God of his fathers.

13 When he prayed to Him, He was moved by his entreaty and heard his supplication, and brought him again to Jerusalem to his kingdom. Then Manasseh knew that the LORD was God.

DISCUSS

• What does God tell you about Manasseh in these verses?

• Look at the *therefore* in verse 11. What is the connection between verse 10 and what happens *therefore*?

• What do you learn about God in verse 13? What effect, if any, does this have on your own view of prayer?

• What was accomplished by prayer, by entreating the Lord?

OBSERVE

Let's see what happened after that.

Leader: *Read 2 Chronicles 33:14–20 aloud.*
  • *Once again have the group underline each reference to **Manasseh**, including pronouns.*

DISCUSS

• What did Manasseh do, and what insights does this give you into the king's relationship to the Lord?

2 CHRONICLES 33:14–20

14 Now after this he built the outer wall of the city of David on the west side of Gihon, in the valley, even to the entrance of the Fish Gate; and he encircled the Ophel with it and made it very high. Then he put army commanders in all the fortified cities of Judah.

15 He also removed the foreign gods and the idol from the house of the LORD, as well as all the altars which he had built on the mountain of the house of the LORD and in Jerusalem, and he threw them outside the city.

16 He set up the altar of the LORD and sacrificed peace offerings and thank offerings on it; and he ordered Judah to serve the LORD God of Israel.

17 Nevertheless the people still sacrificed in the high places, although only to the LORD their God.

18 Now the rest of the acts of Manasseh even his prayer to his God, and the words of the seers who spoke to him in the name of the LORD God of Israel, behold, they are among the records of the kings of Israel.

19 His prayer also and how God was entreated by him, and all his sin, his unfaithfulness, and the sites on which he built high

• Thinking back to the previous passage, what was it that brought this about?

• What do you learn about God in verse 19? What personal encouragement might come from knowing this?

• Have you—or has someone you know—ever experienced a crisis, prayed, and then witnessed God move in answer to prayer? What happened to your relationship with God or to that person's relationship with God, and why?

places and erected the Asherim and the carved images, before he humbled himself, behold, they are written in the records of the Hozai.

20 So Manasseh slept with his fathers, and they buried him in his own house. And Amon his son became king in his place.

OBSERVE

Manasseh's example gave us some indication of the impact sin has on our relationship with God. Sin separates us from God. So what is the solution?

Leader: Read Psalm 32:1–4 aloud. Have the group say aloud and…
• *underline every reference to **the person:** every **he, man, I, me,** and **my.***
• *mark all references to **transgression, sin, iniquity** with a big **X.***

PSALM 32:1–4

1 How blessed is he whose transgression is forgiven, whose sin is covered!

2 How blessed is the man to whom the LORD does not impute iniquity, and in whose spirit there is no deceit!

3 When I kept silent about my sin, my body wasted away through my groaning all day long.

4 For day and night Your hand was heavy upon me; my vitality was drained away as with the fever heat of summer. Selah.

PSALM 32:5–11

5 I acknowledged my sin to You, and my iniquity I did not hide; I said, "I will confess my transgressions to the LORD"; and You forgave the guilt of my sin. Selah.

6 Therefore, let everyone who is godly pray to You in a time when You may be

DISCUSS

• Verse 4 ends with *Selah,* which means to pause and reflect on what was written. So pause now and look at where you've marked the text. Discuss the situation of this person. What is his problem? What happened to this person, to his body, and why?

OBSERVE

Leader: Read Psalm 32:5–11 aloud. Have the group do the following:

• *Underline every reference to **the person:** every **I, me,** and **my.***
• *Mark all references to **transgression, sin, iniquity** with a big **X.***
• *Put a triangle over the references to **the Lord,** including pronouns.*
• *Mark **prayer** like this:* (prayer)

DISCUSS

• What did this person do in regard to his sin? How did the Lord respond?

• Verse 6 begins with "therefore," which is a term of conclusion. What preceded leads to a point of understanding. So what is the application to the reader of this psalm?

• How did the psalmist feel about God? What did he say about Him, and what effect did this have on his spirit?

• What did God tell the psalmist He would do?

• Why do you think God made this promise?

• Do you see passion ignited in the psalmist and in others who trust in the Lord? If so, what is the evidence and what is the driving factor? (Don't miss how such people are described in verse 11.)

found; Surely in a flood of great waters they will not reach him.

7 You are my hiding place; You preserve me from trouble; You surround me with songs of deliverance. Selah.

8 I will instruct you and teach you in the way which you should go; I will counsel you with My eye upon you.

9 Do not be as the horse or as the mule which have no understanding, whose trappings include bit and bridle to hold them in check, otherwise they will not come near to you.

10 Many are the sorrows of the wicked, but

he who trusts in the
LORD, lovingkindness
shall surround him.

¹¹ Be glad in the LORD
and rejoice, you right-
eous ones; and shout for
joy, all you who are
upright in heart.

• How could you use this psalm to help
someone who feels far from God—
empty, spiritually down, numb towards
the Lord and the things of the Lord?

JOHN 15:1–10, 16

¹ I am the true vine,
and My Father is the
vinedresser.

² Every branch in
Me that does not bear
fruit, He takes away;
and every branch that
bears fruit, He prunes
it so that it may bear
more fruit.

³ You are already
clean because of the
word which I have
spoken to you.

OBSERVE

If anything ought to stir our hearts and
increase our passion for God, it would be
to know that He not only hears us when
we pray, but He answers!

*Leader: Read John 15:1–10, 16. Have the
group do the following:*

- *Mark all references to **Jesus,** including
  pronouns, with a cross:* †
- *Underline each occurrence of **you** in
  reference to the disciples and any pronoun that refers to **one who abides.***
- *Circle each occurrence of the word
  abide(s).*
- *Mark the word **ask** like this:* ⟨ask⟩

INSIGHT

The Greek word translated here as *abide* is *meno*. It means "to dwell, remain, to make your home in, to stay (abide) in a given state." In verse 4, *abide* is an aorist imperative verb, which means it is a command.

DISCUSS

• What did you learn from marking the references to Jesus? What is His relationship to the Father and to believers?

• What do you learn about the branches that abide in Jesus?

• According to verses 9–10, what are we to abide in and how is that done?

⁴ Abide in Me, and I in you. As the branch cannot bear fruit of itself unless it abides in the vine, so neither can you unless you abide in Me.

⁵ I am the vine, you are the branches; he who abides in Me and I in him, he bears much fruit, for apart from Me you can do nothing.

⁶ If anyone does not abide in Me, he is thrown away as a branch and dries up; and they gather them, and cast them into the fire and they are burned.

⁷ If you abide in Me, and My words abide in you, ask whatever you wish, and it will be done for you.

8 My Father is glorified by this, that you bear much fruit, and so prove to be My disciples.

9 Just as the Father has loved Me, I have also loved you; abide in My love.

10 If you keep My commandments, you will abide in My love; just as I have kept My Father's commandments and abide in His love....

16 You did not choose Me but I chose you, and appointed you that you would go and bear fruit, and that your fruit would remain, so that whatever you ask of the Father in My name He may give to you.

• What do you learn from marking *ask* in verses 7 and 16? What would be a synonym for *ask*?

• Just to make sure we don't miss anything, what enables us to ask and be confident that God will hear and act in response?

• Practically, how could knowing and obeying the truths of John 15 stir up your passion for the Lord?

WRAP IT UP

Jesus taught that we must abide, dwell, live in Him, and that His words must abide, dwell, live in us. When this happens, whatever we ask will be given to us. E. M. Bounds wrote, "Prayer is the greatest of all forces, because it honors God and brings Him into active aid."*

God wants to answer prayer—but His holiness, His righteousness cannot allow Him to answer us when we knowingly allow sin in our lives and are unwilling to confess it for what it is and forsake it.

John recorded the truth in his gospel: "We know that God does not hear sinners; but if anyone is God-fearing and does His will, He hears him" (John 9:31). When he wrote 1 John, John was moved by the Spirit to tell us that "If we say that we have no sin, we are deceiving ourselves and the truth is not in us" (1:8). But he also assured us, "If we confess our sins, He is faithful and righteous to forgive us our sins and to cleanse us from all unrighteousness" (1:9).

Remember the branches on the vine in John 15? They need pruning to bear greater fruit. So if you want to ignite your passion for the Lord, to sing "songs of deliverance" (Psalm 32:7), if you want to be used of God to confront sin and bring reformation as Manasseh did (2 Chronicles 33:14–20), and if you want to expectantly ask in His name with confidence (John 15:16)—then lift up your "holy hands" and pray (1 Timothy 2:8)!

---

* E. M. Bounds, *The Complete Works of E. M. Bounds on Prayer* (Grand Rapids, MI: Baker, 1990), 317.

You can be assured that when your life and your prayers align with God's will, they will be answered. This is why it is so important to understand and know God's Word for yourself, for when you know it, are abiding in it, *and pray,* you will see God move in ways far beyond what you could ever ask or imagine.

Today when someone mentions worship, our minds often turn to the "worship" part of the church service—the singing of songs or hymns that precedes the sermon. Consequently, depending on our preferences or experience, the word *worship* can stir up all sorts of emotions and debate.

However, according to the Bible, worship involves more than the time of singing during a church service. Worship is both an attitude and an act. The word means "to bow," thus worship is the act of bowing before God to show His worth and value while revealing our attitude of humility.

This week we'll consider the relationship between worship and a vibrant passion for God.

OBSERVE

Let's begin by looking at the first time the Hebrew word *shachah* is translated as *worship* in the Bible.

Leader: Read Genesis 22:1–12, 18 aloud. Have the group say and...
- *underline every reference to **Abraham**, including pronouns.*
- *mark **love** with a heart:* ♡
- *place a check mark over the word **obeyed**, like this:* ✓
- *mark **worship** and **fear** with a big **W**.*

GENESIS 22:1–12, 18

¹ Now it came about after these things, that God tested Abraham, and said to him, "Abraham!" And he said, "Here I am."

² He said, "Take now your son, your only son, whom you love, Isaac, and go to the land of Moriah,

and offer him there as a burnt offering on one of the mountains of which I will tell you."

³ So Abraham rose early in the morning and saddled his donkey, and took two of his young men with him and Isaac his son; and he split wood for the burnt offering, and arose and went to the place of which God had told him.

⁴ On the third day Abraham raised his eyes and saw the place from a distance.

⁵ Abraham said to his young men, "Stay here with the donkey, and I and the lad will go over there; and we

DISCUSS

• According to verse 1, what was God doing to Abraham?

• What do you learn from marking *love*?

• How did Abraham respond to God's instruction?

• Worship is mentioned in verse 5. Describe the context in which it is used. How will Abraham and Isaac worship?

• What do you learn from marking *obeyed*?

• What connection, if any, do you see between these words, many of which are used for the first time in the Word of God in this passage: *love, worship, fear,* and *obey*? (Keep in mind all you have learned during the past three weeks in this study.)

will worship and return to you."

6 Abraham took the wood of the burnt offering and laid it on Isaac his son, and he took in his hand the fire and the knife. So the two of them walked on together.

7 Isaac spoke to Abraham his father and said, "My father!" And he said, "Here I am, my son." And he said, "Behold, the fire and the wood, but where is the lamb for the burnt offering?"

8 Abraham said, "God will provide for Himself the lamb for the burnt offering, my son." So the two of them walked on together.

⁹ Then they came to the place of which God had told him; and Abraham built the altar there and arranged the wood, and bound his son Isaac and laid him on the altar, on top of the wood.

¹⁰ Abraham stretched out his hand and took the knife to slay his son.

¹¹ But the angel of the LORD called to him from heaven and said, "Abraham, Abraham!" And he said, "Here I am."

¹² He said, "Do not stretch out your hand against the lad, and do nothing to him; for now I know that you fear God, since you

INSIGHT

The Hebrew word *shachah*, most often translated *worship* or *bow*, means "to bow down, prostrate oneself." It is used in regard to bowing before a superior in homage, before God in worship, before false gods, and before angels.*

To give homage to another is to respect them, to honor them for who they are or the position they hold. It is similar to fear—respect, trust, honor. The Old Testament language scholar H. F. Fuchs wrote that "fear of God becomes synonymous with reverence, worship and obedience to God's command."**

A simple way to think of worship is to look at God's worth and think and act accordingly.

---

* J. Strong, *Enhanced Strong's Lexicon* (Bellingham, WA: Logos Bible Software, 2001).
** H. F. Fuchs, *Theological Dictionary of the Old Testament*, ed. G. Johannes Botterweck and Helmer Ringgren (Grand Rapids, MI: Eerdmans, 1990), 2:298.

• How does what you've observed in Genesis 22 fit with your understanding of worship?

OBSERVE

In ancient Israel, the ark of the covenant was the primary symbol of God's presence. In 1 Chronicles 15 David brought the ark into Jerusalem with exuberant celebration and led the people in a time of worship. Let's see what we can learn from his words.

Leader: Read 1 Chronicles 16:28–36 aloud, slowly. Have the group…
  • *place a check mark over the word* **ascribe.**
  • *mark* **worship** *with a big* **W**. *It is only used once, but we don't want you to miss it.*
  • *mark* **praise** *with a big* **P.**

have not withheld your son, your only son, from Me....

18 "In your seed all the nations of the earth shall be blessed, because you have obeyed My voice."

1 CHRONICLES 16:28–36

28 Ascribe to the LORD, O families of the peoples, ascribe to the LORD glory and strength.

29 Ascribe to the LORD the glory due His name; bring an offering, and come before Him; worship the LORD in holy array.

30 Tremble before Him, all the earth; indeed, the world is

firmly established, it will not be moved.

31 Let the heavens be glad, and let the earth rejoice; and let them say among the nations, "The LORD reigns."

32 Let the sea roar, and all it contains; let the field exult, and all that is in it.

33 Then the trees of the forest will sing for joy before the LORD; for He is coming to judge the earth.

34 O give thanks to the LORD, for He is good; for His lovingkindness is everlasting.

35 Then say, "Save us, O God of our salvation, and gather us

INSIGHT

The word *ascribe* means "to give credit to the author or source." David directed the people to ascribe glory—honor, a correct estimate, weight, gravity—to God.

True worship is ascribing rightful credit to our holy God, who declares, "I am the LORD, that is My name; I will not give My glory to another, nor My praise to graven images" (Isaiah 42:8).

DISCUSS

• The exhortation to worship the Lord in holy array, or attire, also is found in 2 Chronicles 20:21 and in Psalm 29:2; 96:9. There are differing interpretations of the phrase, and no one is exactly sure what it means to worship in holy attire. However, if we would ascribe to the Lord the glory due His name, how would it affect the way we worship, including the way we dress when we worship Him?

• If we don't want to distract others around us from worshiping the Lord and our desire is to give all glory to Him, how might that impact our choice of attire?

and deliver us from the nations, to give thanks to Your holy name, and glory in Your praise."

36 Blessed be the LORD, the God of Israel, from everlasting even to everlasting. Then all the people said, "Amen," and praised the LORD.

OBSERVE

After a thorough explanation of the gospel of Jesus Christ, Paul wrote Romans 12:1–2. This passage begins with "therefore," which, as we've seen, is a term of conclusion. Let's look at that conclusion.

Leader: Read Romans 12:1–2 aloud. Have the group say and...
   • *underline* **brethren** *and every* **you** *and* **your**.
   • *mark* **worship** *with a big* **W**.

ROMANS 12:1–2

1 Therefore I urge you, brethren, by the mercies of God, to present your bodies a living and holy sacrifice, acceptable to God, which is your spiritual service of worship.

² And do not be conformed to this world, but be transformed by the renewing of your mind, so that you may prove what the will of God is, that which is good and acceptable and perfect.

DISCUSS

• What did Paul urge the brethren, believers, to do in verse 1?

• What reason did he give?

• So what do you learn about worship in Romans 12:1?

• What instruction do you find in verse 2?

INSIGHT

The word *conformed* is translated from the Greek *suschematizo (syschematizo)* and means "to fashion alike." It could be described as being squeezed into a mold.

The Greek word translated here as *transformed* is *metamorphoo,* which means "transformed, changed, transfigured." Think of a caterpillar becoming a butterfly.

• According to verse 2, how is this transformation accomplished?

• What happens as a result? What is the benefit, the end result of being transformed? What are we then able to do?

• What does God tell you through the apostle Paul about His will?

• Do you really believe that? Why or why not?

• Did you notice that Paul urged the readers of this letter to worship God in this way? How might worshiping like this demonstrate or impact your passion for the Lord?

62   Ignite Your Passion for God

JOHN 4:19–24

19 The woman said to Him, "Sir, I perceive that You are a prophet.

20 "Our fathers worshiped in this mountain, and you people say that in Jerusalem is the place where men ought to worship."

21 Jesus said to her, "Woman, believe Me, an hour is coming when neither in this mountain nor in Jerusalem will you worship the Father.

22 "You worship what you do not know; we worship what we know, for salvation is from the Jews.

23 "But an hour is coming, and now is,

OBSERVE

Let's join a dialogue between Jesus and a Samaritan woman at Jacob's well. Jesus has just told her that He knows she has had five husbands and the man she is living with now is not her husband. Note how she responds.

Leader: Read John 4:19–24.
  • *Have the group mark **worship** with a* **W.**

DISCUSS

• Who brings up the subject of worship, and what point is that person making?

• How did Jesus respond? What do you learn about worship from His response?

• What does a true worshiper do, and why?

• So what does this tell you about worship?

• According to Jesus, what is the Father looking for?

• What do you think that kind of worship would look like in a person's life?

• Would you qualify? Why or why not?

OBSERVE

Leader: Read Philippians 3:3 aloud.
  • *Have the group mark* ***worship*** *with a* **W.**

DISCUSS

• The true circumcision Paul wrote of is that of the heart, the removal of a heart of stone and the receiving of a heart of flesh. In other words, he was describing those who are under the new covenant of grace rather than under the Law. So how does such a person worship?

when the true worshipers will worship the Father in spirit and truth; for such people the Father seeks to be His worshipers.

24 "God is spirit, and those who worship Him must worship in spirit and truth."

PHILIPPIANS 3:3

For we are the true circumcision, who worship in the Spirit of God and glory in Christ Jesus and put no confidence in the flesh.

• What connection, if any, do you see here with what Jesus said to the woman in John 4? Explain your answer.

REVELATION 5:7–14

7 And He [Jesus] came and took the book out of the right hand of Him who sat on the throne.

8 When He had taken the book, the four living creatures and the twenty-four elders fell down before the Lamb, each one holding a harp and golden bowls full of incense, which are the prayers of the saints.

9 And they sang a new song, saying, "Worthy are You to take the book and to break its seals; for You

OBSERVE

Leader: Read Revelation 5:7–14 aloud. Have the group…

• *mark every reference to **Jesus**, including pronouns and synonyms such as **Lamb**, with a cross:* †

• *put a cloud around **worthy**, like this:*

• *mark **worship** with a big* **W.**

DISCUSS

• What did you learn about Jesus in this passage?

• Why is He worthy of worship?

• Just so you don't miss it, according to verse 9 what specific act of Jesus deserves praise?

• What are the results of this action?

were slain, and pur-chased for God with Your blood men from every tribe and tongue and people and nation.

10 "You have made them to be a kingdom and priests to our God; and they will reign upon the earth."

11 Then I looked, and I heard the voice of many angels around the throne and the living creatures and the elders; and the number of them was myriads of myri-ads, and thousands of thousands,

12 saying with a loud voice, "Worthy is the Lamb that was slain to receive power and riches and

wisdom and might and honor and glory and blessing."

13 And every created thing which is in heaven and on the earth and under the earth and on the sea, and all things in them, I heard saying, "To Him who sits on the throne, and to the Lamb, be blessing and honor and glory and dominion forever and ever."

14 And the four living creatures kept saying, "Amen." And the elders fell down and worshiped.

• Look back at 1 Chronicles 16:28–36, which we studied earlier this week. How does this passage relate to what you see in Revelation 5:9–14?

• How does what you've observed in this lesson help shape your understanding of what it means to worship?

WRAP IT UP

As you look at your society, the culture in which you live, do you see many who have destroyed their lives? Have you asked why? What was missing from their lives that they pursued money, power, fame, sex, drugs, alcohol, their happiness, their goals at the expense of others?

Would they have done so if they had walked in the fear of the Lord, if they had pursued the knowledge of God, the wisdom of God rather than the wisdom of this world that scorns the Lord's authority?

In many nations, celebrity in its varied forms often becomes the standard for those who imitate the dress, walk, talk, actions, and lifestyle of famous personalities. Somehow celebrity equates to authority, so the media asks celebrities to weigh in on various issues. And the nations listen to them rather than to God. The Bible is laid aside as irrelevant while humans become the measure of what's right and wrong.

Oh, how we need to realize that God has spoken. In Psalm 2 and elsewhere He has shown His authority and sovereign rule over this world. While many continue to devise plans to elevate themselves to authority and power, they fail to recognize that there is only One who has all power, all authority, and who is worthy of our praise. The nations have lost the fear of the Lord. They rule outside of God's laws and commands. They scheme and devise their plans in vain.

Now those who fear the Lord are opposed, mocked, and often silenced by intimidation. The will and whims of a society made up of varied beliefs often opposed to the Word of God is honored above the truths found in Scripture. Those who don't believe in God nor honor the Bible as God's Word seem to want to obliterate even the mention of His name and the precepts of His Word from society.

You got a glimpse of what God says about Himself in the second lesson in this study. What will the Sovereign God do in and to the nations if this continues? The result of these choices will impact the world.

So can you do anything? Yes. As you finish each lesson, review what you've learned. Think about it. You are studying the Word of God—truth. According to Jesus Christ, it is truth that keeps you from the Evil One, that sets you apart, that teaches you the fear of the Lord.

> And you are not to fear what they fear or be in dread of it.
> It is the LORD of hosts whom you should regard as holy.
> And He shall be your fear,
> And He shall be your dread. (Isaiah 8:12–13)

So learn the fear of the Lord, live in the fear of the Lord, and teach the fear of the Lord to others. If they listen, continue. If they don't, shake the dust off your feet and find those who will. Listen to Jesus:

> I have given them Your word; and the world has hated them, because they are not of the world, even as I am not of the world. I do not ask You to take them out of the world, but to keep them from the evil one. They are not of the world, even as I am not of the world. Sanctify them in the truth; Your word is truth. As You sent Me into the world, I also have sent them into the world. (John 17:14–18)

So go into the world and worship God boldly. If you've placed your trust in Him, what can mere man do to you (Psalm 56:4)?

Do you have a difficult time telling others about Jesus Christ? Is it because you have no real desire to do so? Or perhaps you are afraid of how people might respond, worried somehow you will mess things up?

Oh beloved, wait until you see the truths in this lesson. It could really light your fire!

OBSERVE

Jesus' public witness and ministry was finished. He had proven that He was the Son of God. His hour had come! The grain of wheat had to fall into the ground and die so it would bear much fruit (John 12:24). But before this happened, Jesus had some final truths to share with His disciples. Let's see what we can learn that will help us better share with others the good news of Jesus, the Christ.

Leader: Read John 14:2–3, 16–17 aloud. Have the group…

- *put a cross over every reference to **Jesus**, beginning with **My** in verse 2.*
- *underline every **you**.*
- *mark **Helper** and related pronouns and synonyms with a big **S.***

DISCUSS

- Where did Jesus say He was going, and what would He be doing there?

JOHN 14:2–3, 16–17

2 In My Father's house are many dwelling places; if it were not so, I would have told you; for I go to prepare a place for you.

3 If I go and prepare a place for you, I will come again and receive you to Myself, that

where I am, there you may be also....

16 I will ask the Father, and He will give you another Helper, that He may be with you forever;

17 that is the Spirit of truth, whom the world cannot receive, because it does not see Him or know Him, but you know Him because He abides with you and will be in you.

JOHN 16:7–11

7 But I tell you the truth, it is to your advantage that I go away; for if I do not go away, the Helper will not come to you; but if I go, I will send Him to you.

• What would Jesus ask His Father to do for His followers?

• What did Jesus tell them about the Helper? Don't miss a detail.

• Who cannot receive the Helper, the Spirit of truth, and why?

• When the Helper, the Spirit, comes where will He be?

OBSERVE

So Jesus said He would send the Helper, who "will be in you." And what will the Spirit do?

As you read these next verses, remember that what is promised goes beyond the first disciples who were listening to this. These truths also are for us, because every true believer receives the same Helper, the indwelling Spirit of God (Romans 8:9).

Leader: Read John 16:7–11 aloud. Have the group…
  - *put a cross over every reference to **Jesus**, beginning with **I** in verse 7.*
  - *underline every **you** and **your**.*
  - *mark **Helper** and related pronouns with a big **S**.*

DISCUSS

- Why was it advantageous for Jesus' followers that He go away?

- When Jesus sends the Helper, what three things will the Holy Spirit do?

- Just so you don't miss it, where did Jesus say He would send the Helper? And what does this tell you about God's purpose for you in the world?

8 And He, when He comes, will convict the world concerning sin and righteousness and judgment;

9 concerning sin, because they do not believe in Me;

10 and concerning righteousness, because I go to the Father and you no longer see Me;

11 and concerning judgment, because the ruler of this world has been judged.

INSIGHT

Remember, Jesus came not to condemn the world (they are already condemned because of their sin) but to seek and to save the lost. Although Jesus was leaving, the Father didn't want the world to be without a witness. Therefore the Spirit of God would indwell the eleven—and all people who believe in Jesus Christ. The Spirit in us then will witness to the world so His sheep might hear His voice and be saved, and so that those who do not believe will be without excuse, because they heard the truth and refused to believe.

Thus the Spirit of God lives in us, enabling us to live righteously. He also will witness through us to tell others the gospel so they can believe in Jesus, live righteously, and be freed from Satan's power.

Jesus' death crushed Satan's head (Genesis 3:15) and took away Satan's power of death, because Jesus paid for our sins in full, once for all (Hebrews 2:14–15; 10:10, 14–18). This is the good news the Spirit witnesses to the world through us.

OBSERVE

When Jesus Christ rose from the dead, He spent forty days teaching the eleven disciples (Judas had betrayed Jesus, then hung himself) about the things of the kingdom of God. Then He left to be with the Father and to prepare a place for us before He comes to take us to be with Him.

What were His final orders to the eleven—and to all of us who are to carry on His ministry? Let's see what Luke tells us under the inspiration of the Spirit.

Leader: Read Luke 24:44–49. Have the group…

- *put a cross over every reference to **Jesus**, beginning with the pronoun **He**.*
- *underline any reference to **the eleven disciples**, watching carefully for **them** and **you**.*
- *put a big **S** over **promise** as it is a reference to **the Spirit**, the Helper.*

DISCUSS

- What are Jesus' instructions in these verses?

LUKE 24:44–49

44 Now He said to them, "These are My words which I spoke to you while I was still with you, that all things which are written about Me in the Law of Moses and the Prophets and the Psalms must be fulfilled."

45 Then He opened their minds to understand the Scriptures,

46 and He said to them, "Thus it is written, that the Christ would suffer and rise again from the dead the third day,

47 and that repentance for forgiveness of sins would be proclaimed in His name

to all the nations, beginning from Jerusalem.

48 "You are witnesses of these things.

49 "And behold, I am sending forth the promise of My Father upon you; but you are to stay in the city until you are clothed with power from on high."

ACTS 1:4–9

4 Gathering them together, He commanded them not to leave Jerusalem, but to wait for what the Father had promised, "Which," He said, "you heard of from Me;

5 for John baptized with water, but you

• What is to be proclaimed and where?

• By whom is it to be proclaimed? What will help them to do so?

• Just so you don't miss it, what does Jesus tell His followers to do in verse 49, and what does He promise them?

OBSERVE

Leader: Read Acts 1:4–9 aloud. Have the group...

• *underline every reference to **the eleven disciples,** beginning with **them** in verse 4.*

• *mark all references to **the Holy Spirit,** including the phrase **what the Father had promised,** with a big **S**.*

DISCUSS

• Beginning at verse 4 what do you learn from marking the references to the Spirit?

• When would they receive power, and what would be the result?

• How far would this take them?

will be baptized with the Holy Spirit not many days from now."

6 So when they had come together, they were asking Him, saying, "Lord, is it at this time You are restoring the kingdom to Israel?"

7 He said to them, "It is not for you to know times or epochs which the Father has fixed by His own authority;

8 but you will receive power when the Holy Spirit has come upon you; and you shall be My witnesses both in Jerusalem, and in all Judea and Samaria, and even to the

remotest part of the earth."

⁹ And after He had said these things, He was lifted up while they were looking on, and a cloud received Him out of their sight.

• Think about what you've learned so far in this week's study. Since the eleven disciples saw Jesus leave, what could they expect?

Acts 3:1–10

¹ Now Peter and John were going up to the temple at the ninth hour, the hour of prayer.

² And a man who had been lame from his mother's womb was being carried along, whom they used to set down every day at the gate of the temple which is called Beautiful, in order

OBSERVE

Acts 2 records how the Helper, the Holy Spirit, came—just as Jesus had promised! Let's move on to Acts 3 to learn what happened after the Spirit came and see what lessons we find for our lives.

Leader: Read Acts 3:1–10 aloud slowly, so the story can be enjoyed. Have the group...
  • *underline all the references to **Peter** and **John**, two of Jesus' apostles/disciples.*
  • *put a check mark over the reference to **the man** who is first mentioned in verse 2.*

DISCUSS

• Describe the interaction between the man and the disciples, Peter and John.

• What was the man's situation and what did he want from Peter and John?

to beg alms of those who were entering the temple.

3 When he saw Peter and John about to go into the temple, he began asking to receive alms.

4 But Peter, along with John, fixed his gaze on him and said, "Look at us!"

5 And he began to give them his attention, expecting to receive something from them.

6 But Peter said, "I do not possess silver and gold, but what I do have I give to you: In the name of Jesus Christ the Nazarene—walk!"

7 And seizing him by the right hand, he raised him up; and immediately his feet and his ankles were strengthened.

8 With a leap he stood upright and began to walk; and he entered the temple with them, walking and leaping and praising God.

9 And all the people saw him walking and praising God;

10 and they were taking note of him as being the one who used to sit at the Beautiful Gate of the temple to beg alms, and they were filled with wonder and amazement at what had happened to him.

• How did Peter respond?

• What happened next? Don't miss a single detail.

OBSERVE

Leader: Read Acts 3:11–20 aloud. Have the group...

- *underline the references to **Peter**.*
- *circle the references to **the people** and to **men of Israel**, including pronouns and synonyms such as **brethren**.*
- *put a cross over every reference to **Jesus**, including synonyms and pronouns.*

DISCUSS

- Describe what Peter was doing in these verses.

- Who was Peter addressing? What do you learn about this group from the text?

ACTS 3:11–20

11 While he was clinging to Peter and John, all the people ran together to them at the so-called portico of Solomon, full of amazement.

12 But when Peter saw this, he replied to the people, "Men of Israel, why are you amazed at this, or why do you gaze at us, as if by our own power or piety we had made him walk?

13 "The God of Abraham, Isaac and Jacob, the God of our fathers, has glorified His servant Jesus, the one whom you delivered and disowned in the presence of Pilate, when

he had decided to release Him.

14 "But you disowned the Holy and Righteous One and asked for a murderer to be granted to you,

15 but put to death the Prince of life, the one whom God raised from the dead, a fact to which we are witnesses.

16 "And on the basis of faith in His name, it is the name of Jesus which has strengthened this man whom you see and know; and the faith which comes through Him has given him this perfect health in the presence of you all.

17 "And now, brethren, I know that

• What did Peter tell them about Jesus?

• Do you think his words might have left them feeling convicted? Explain your answer.

• Look at verses 19 and 20. What did Peter urge the people to do, and why?

• Do you think Peter was fired up? If so, what was the reason for his passion?

• If you can, describe a time when you found yourself in a specific situation that you used to share the good news about Jesus Christ. How did you feel afterward?

you acted in ignorance, just as your rulers did also.

18 "But the things which God announced beforehand by the mouth of all the prophets, that His Christ would suffer, He has thus fulfilled.

19 "Therefore repent and return, so that your sins may be wiped away, in order that times of refreshing may come from the presence of the Lord;

20 and that He may send Jesus, the Christ appointed for you."

ACTS 4:1–4

¹ As they were speaking to the people, the priests and the captain of the temple guard and the Sadducees came up to them,

² being greatly disturbed because they were teaching the people and proclaiming in Jesus the resurrection from the dead.

³ And they laid hands on them and put them in jail until the next day, for it was already evening.

⁴ But many of those who had heard the message believed; and the number of the men came to be about five thousand.

OBSERVE

Peter's message did not go unnoticed by the religious leaders. Let's see how they responded.

Leader: Read Acts 4:1–4 aloud. Have the group do the following:

- *Underline the references to **Peter** and **John**.*
- *Put a semicircle over **the various groups** that come up to Peter and John, like this:* ⌒
- *Circle the references to **the people who heard the message.***
- *Put a cross over any reference to **Jesus**.*

DISCUSS

- What happened to Peter and John, and why?

- What happened to some of the people who heard Peter's message?

- Why didn't the priests, the temple captain, and the Sadducees like Peter's message?

OBSERVE

The story is not over. Let's see what happened the following morning.

Leader: Read Acts 4:5–13 aloud and have the group do the following:
- *Put a semicircle over the various* **groups of people** *mentioned in the text.*
- *Underline the references to* **Peter** *and* **John***.*
- *Mark all references to* **the Spirit** *with a big* **S***.*
- *Put a cross over every reference to* **Jesus***. (Be sure to mark* **no one else** *in verse 12 so you don't miss Jesus!)*

DISCUSS

- What did Peter say about Jesus Christ?

ACTS 4:5–13

5 On the next day, their rulers and elders and scribes were gathered together in Jerusalem;

6 and Annas the high priest was there, and Caiaphas and John and Alexander, and all who were of high-priestly descent.

7 When they had placed them in the center, they began to inquire, "By what power, or in what name, have you done this?"

8 Then Peter, filled with the Holy Spirit, said to them, "Rulers and elders of the people,

9 if we are on trial today for a benefit done to a sick man, as to how this man has been made well,

10 let it be known to all of you and to all the people of Israel, that by the name of Jesus Christ the Nazarene, whom you crucified, whom God raised from the dead— by this name this man stands here before you in good health.

11 "He is the stone which was rejected by you, the builders, but which became the chief corner stone.

12 "And there is salvation in no one else; for there is no other name under heaven that has been given among men by which we must be saved."

13 Now as they observed the confidence of Peter and

• What does verse 12 tell you about all other religions, philosophies, and beliefs about life after death?

• So if you know this, what is your responsibility?

• What do you learn about Peter in verse 8?

• How are Peter and John described in verse 13?

• How might knowing all this help you when you are led by God to share the gospel?

John and understood that they were uneducated and untrained men, they were amazed, and began to recognize them as having been with Jesus.

OBSERVE

What if others forbid you to share what God says in His Word? What if they want to shut you up, even put you in jail? Let's see what Peter and John can teach us about how to respond.

Leader: Read Acts 4:15–20 aloud. Have the group…
- *put a semicircle over the pronouns that refer to the members of the Council.*
- *underline every reference to Peter and John.*

DISCUSS

• The Council was a group of men who ruled the Jews under the authority of Rome. What were their instructions in verse 18?

ACTS 4:15–20

15 But when they had ordered them to leave the Council, they began to confer with one another,

16 saying, "What shall we do with these men? For the fact that a noteworthy miracle has taken place through them is apparent to all who live in Jerusalem, and we cannot deny it.

17 "But so that it will not spread any further among the people, let us warn them to speak

no longer to any man in this name."

18 And when they had summoned them, they commanded them not to speak or teach at all in the name of Jesus.

19 But Peter and John answered and said to them, "Whether it is right in the sight of God to give heed to you rather than to God, you be the judge;

20 for we cannot stop speaking about what we have seen and heard."

2 TIMOTHY 4:1–5

1 I solemnly charge you in the presence of God and of Christ Jesus, who is to judge the living and the dead, and by His

• How did Peter and John respond?

• What does spiritual passion look like?

• Describe how you've observed spiritual passion in someone's life and how it affected others around them.

Leader: If you don't have time for this next scripture, urge the class to study it at home and make it their prayer this week.

OBSERVE

We have a final charge from God's Word regarding the importance of sharing the gospel.

Leader: Read 2 Timothy 4:1–5 aloud with the group. Have the group . . .

  • *place a check mark over every **instruction** given by Paul in this passage.*

DISCUSS

• What is the pivotal charge from Paul in this passage? Looking specifically at verse 2, what are believers to do?

• What sort of response should we anticipate?

• What does verse 5 suggest about our responsibility when others resist sound doctrine?

Leader: If time permits, pray about this charge and all that you've learned this week.

appearing and His kingdom:

2 preach the word; be ready in season and out of season; reprove, rebuke, exhort, with great patience and instruction.

3 For the time will come when they will not endure sound doctrine; but wanting to have their ears tickled, they will accumulate for themselves teachers in accordance to their own desires,

4 and will turn away their ears from the truth and will turn aside to myths.

5 But you, be sober in all things, endure hardship, do the work of an evangelist, fulfill your ministry.

WRAP IT UP

Sharing the good news of Jesus Christ with others is the end result of getting rid of idols, being in God's Word, spending time in prayer, and worshiping Him in spirit and truth. When we're fully engaged with God and all that He's doing, like Peter and John "we cannot stop speaking about what we have seen and heard" (Acts 4:20).

Sharing the Word—teaching others about Jesus through the indwelling power of the Holy Spirit—will further fuel your passion. And as you, beloved of God, remain a faithful witness to Jesus even in the face of persecution, you can know that you will be unashamed when you see Him face to face.

The marathon is a grueling 26.2 mile, or 42.2 km, test of mind, body, and strength. Some may wonder why anyone would put themselves through that. But experienced athletes know that to run that final mile and cross the finish line, to earn a shiny gold medal and the title of marathon runner is worth all the pain and suffering. In other words, the reward makes it worth the pain.

Like a marathon, the Christian life includes highs and lows, times when you feel great, and times when you really suffer. When we face suffering and persecution we can either become like a turtle that retreats into his shell for protection or view our suffering as an opportunity to glorify God.

In this final week we'll look at a few godly men to see how suffering for the gospel ignites our passion for God.

OBSERVE

First we need to understand the why of suffering for the gospel. Jesus explained as He sent out the twelve disciples and warned them of what they were about to face.

Leader: *Read Matthew 10:16–23 aloud and have the group…*
  * *draw a cross over references to **Jesus,** who is speaking in this passage. Be sure to include synonyms and pronouns.*
  * *underline every **you** and **your,** which refer to **the disciples.***

MATTHEW 10:16–23

16 Behold, I send you out as sheep in the midst of wolves; so be shrewd as serpents and innocent as doves.

17 But beware of men, for they will ①hand you over to the courts and scourge you in their synagogues;

18 and you will even be brought before governors and kings for My sake, as a testimony to them and to the Gentiles.

19 But when they hand you over, do not worry about how or what you are to say; for it will be given you in that hour what you are to say.

20 For it is not you who speak, but it is the Spirit of your Father who speaks in you.

21 Brother will betray brother to death, and a father his child; and children will rise up against parents and cause them to be put to death.

22 You will be hated by all because of My name, but it is the one

Leader: *Have the group read through the text again, verse by verse. As you do, number each action that will be taken against believers. We've marked the first one for you.*

DISCUSS
• What did you learn from numbering the actions believers should expect to endure?

• Why will believers face suffering and persecution, according to Jesus?

• What promise did Jesus give to the one who endures to the end?

• Do you see believers suffering like this today? Are you facing persecution for your faith? Explain your answer.

• How do you respond when facing challenges to your faith?

OBSERVE

In the days of the early church, many Jewish believers left Judea due to persecution from the Roman Empire for their testimony in Jesus. In light of this persecution James addressed how the believers were to respond to suffering.

Leader: Read James 1:1–8, 12 aloud and have the group mark…

• *every reference to **trials**, including synonyms, with a jagged line, like this:*

~~~~

• ***faith** with an open book, like this:*

📖

who has endured to the end who will be saved.

23 But whenever they persecute you in one city, flee to the next; for truly I say to you, you will not finish going through the cities of Israel until the Son of Man comes.

JAMES 1:1–8, 12

1 James, a bond-servant of God and of the Lord Jesus Christ, To the twelve tribes who are dispersed abroad: Greetings.

2 Consider it all joy, my brethren, when you encounter various trials,

3 knowing that the testing of your faith produces endurance.

4 And let endurance have its perfect result, so that you may be perfect and complete, lacking in nothing.

5 But if any of you lacks wisdom, let him ask of God, who gives to all generously and without reproach, and it will be given to him.

6 But he must ask in faith without any doubting, for the one who doubts is like the surf of the sea, driven and tossed by the wind.

7 For that man ought not to expect that he will receive anything from the Lord,

8 being a double-minded man, unstable in all his ways....

DISCUSS

• How does James call the believers to respond to trials and suffering?

• In verse 3 James said that the testing of our faith produces endurance. How does responding in joy strengthen our faith?

INSIGHT

"Consider it all joy" (verse 2) can also be translated "count it all joy." The natural response to suffering and persecution is to complain, but believers must make a conscious effort to face trials and suffering with joy. When we respond in this way, knowing that trials are producing in us endurance, the result is perfection; not a sinless perfection but a spiritual maturity that produces a deeper communion with and greater trust in Jesus Christ.

• What did James say about the man who perseveres under trial? How does knowing this truth change your mind toward suffering for the gospel?

12 Blessed is a man who perseveres under trial; for once he has been approved, he will receive the crown of life which the Lord has promised to those who love Him.

OBSERVE

As we saw last week, the book of Acts describes the early days of the church, when the gospel was being preached and thousands were added to the church. The high priest and his Council tried to silence the apostles and prevent them from teaching about Jesus. We pick up the story in Acts 5:27 as Peter and the apostles were brought before the high priest and the Council to face questions over why they continued to preach.

ACTS 5:27–35, 38–42

27 When they had brought them, they stood them before the Council. The high priest questioned them,

28 saying, "We gave you strict orders not to continue teaching in this name, and yet, you have filled Jerusalem with your teaching and intend to bring this man's blood upon us."

29 But Peter and the apostles answered, "We must obey God rather than men.

30 "The God of our fathers raised up Jesus, whom you had put to death by hanging Him on a cross.

31 "He is the one whom God exalted to His right hand as a Prince and a Savior, to grant repentance to Israel, and forgiveness of sins.

32 "And we are witnesses of these things; and so is the Holy Spirit, whom God has given to those who obey Him."

33 But when they heard this, they were cut to the quick

Leader: Read aloud Acts 5:27–35, 38–42 and have the group…

- *underline references to **Peter** and **the apostles**.*
- *put a big **V** over every reference to **witnesses, teaching, speak,** and **preaching**.*
- *mark **flogged** and **suffer** with a jagged line:* 〰️

DISCUSS

- How did the apostles answer the questioning from the Council?

- What was Peter doing in verses 29–32?

- How did the Council respond?

• What happened to Peter and the apostles as a result of their witness? Why?

• How does this relate to Jesus' words in Matthew 10, which you read at the beginning of this lesson?

• After being beaten (flogged), how did the apostles respond?

• Did the suffering smother the fire of their passion? How do you know?

and intended to kill them.

34 But a Pharisee named Gamaliel, a teacher of the Law, respected by all the people, stood up in the Council and gave orders to put the men outside for a short time.

35 And he said to them, "Men of Israel, take care what you propose to do with these men....

38 "So in the present case, I say to you, stay away from these men and let them alone, for if this plan or action is of men, it will be overthrown;

39 but if it is of God, you will not be able to overthrow them; or

else you may even be found fighting against God."

40 They took his advice; and after calling the apostles in, they flogged them and ordered them not to speak in the name of Jesus, and then released them.

41 So they went on their way from the presence of the Council, rejoicing that they had been considered worthy to suffer shame for His name.

42 And every day, in the temple and from house to house, they kept right on teaching and preaching Jesus as the Christ.

• How does this example shed light on the passage we studied in James?

• Put yourself in the sandals of the apostles: how would you have responded in this situation?

OBSERVE

The apostle Paul knew a lot about suffering for the gospel.

Leader: Read 2 Corinthians 1:5–10 aloud and have the group…
- *mark* **sufferings, afflicted** *with a jagged line:* /\\\\/\\V
- *put a big* **C** *over each reference to* **comfort** *or* **comforted.**
- *mark each reference to* **God,** *including pronouns, with a triangle.*

DISCUSS

- What did you learn from marking the words *sufferings* and *afflicted*?

- What did you learn from marking *comfort* or *comforted*?

- Look a little closer at verse 5. When we share in the sufferings of Christ, for His sake what do we receive in abundance?

- What did you learn from marking the references to God?

2 CORINTHIANS 1:5–10

5 For just as the sufferings of Christ are ours in abundance, so also our comfort is abundant through Christ.

6 But if we are afflicted, it is for your comfort and salvation; or if we are comforted, it is for your comfort, which is effective in the patient enduring of the same sufferings which we also suffer;

7 and our hope for you is firmly grounded, knowing that as you are sharers of our sufferings, so also you are sharers of our comfort.

8 For we do not want you to be unaware, brethren, of

our affliction which came to us in Asia, that we were burdened excessively, beyond our strength, so that we despaired even of life;

9 indeed, we had the sentence of death within ourselves so that we would not trust in ourselves, but in God who raises the dead;

10 who delivered us from so great a peril of death, and will deliver us, He on whom we have set our hope. And He will yet deliver us.

2 CORINTHIANS 11:24–28

24 Five times I received from the Jews thirty-nine lashes.

25 Three times I was beaten with rods, once

INSIGHT

The word *comfort,* used ten times in 2 Corinthians 1:1-7, literally means "to call to one's side." In verses 3 and 4 we read that the "God of all comfort...comforts us in all our affliction." What joy for us to know that God is at our side when we face suffering and affliction for His sake!

• How does knowing that God is at your side in the midst of suffering and persecution ignite your passion for Him?

• When Paul wrote of being delivered, was he referring to a temporal deliverance from his current trial or was he pointing to an eternal hope or future deliverance? Explain your answer.

• To what extent was Paul willing to suffer for the gospel? (Hint: Look at verse 9.)

OBSERVE

Let's take a quick look at Paul's personal sufferings which he mentioned in 2 Corinthians 11.

Leader: *Read 2 Corinthians 11:24-28 aloud.*
• *Have the group underline each **affliction** and **suffering** Paul experienced.*

DISCUSS

• What different types of suffering and afflictions did Paul experience for the gospel?

• What other sources of pressure did Paul face, aside from the persecutions and afflictions?

• Was Paul an extraordinary man that he could handle all of these struggles? Explain your answer.

• How would you respond if you were in Paul's sandals?

I was stoned, three times I was shipwrecked, a night and a day I have spent in the deep.

26 I have been on frequent journeys, in dangers from rivers, dangers from robbers, dangers from my countrymen, dangers from the Gentiles, dangers in the city, dangers in the wilderness, dangers on the sea, dangers among false brethren;

27 I have been in labor and hardship, through many sleepless nights, in hunger and thirst, often without food, in cold and exposure.

28 Apart from such external things, there is the daily pressure on me of concern for all the churches.

2 CORINTHIANS 4:7–18

7 But we have this treasure in earthen vessels, so that the surpassing greatness of the power will be of God and not from ourselves;

8 we are afflicted in every way, but not crushed; perplexed, but not despairing;

9 persecuted, but not forsaken; struck down, but not destroyed;

10 always carrying about in the body the dying of Jesus, so that the life of Jesus also may be manifested in our body.

11 For we who live are constantly being delivered over to death

OBSERVE

Second Corinthians 4:7–18 gives us even greater insight into how Paul could rejoice in suffering for the gospel.

Leader: Read 2 Corinthians 4:7–18 and have the group...
- *underline every reference to **the suffering believers,** including pronouns such as **we** and **us.***
- *mark with a jagged line all **the ways they suffered.***

DISCUSS

- What were the various ways these believers suffered? Discuss them.

- Look at verse 7. What is the "treasure" to which Paul refers, and how might it motivate believers to press on through persecution?

• What explanation did Paul give for why he could respond to suffering in this way?

for Jesus' sake, so that the life of Jesus also may be manifested in our mortal flesh.

12 So death works in us, but life in you.

13 But having the same spirit of faith, according to what is written, "I believed, therefore I spoke," we also believe, therefore we also speak,

• As you look at verses 12 and 15, what motivation do you see for sharing the gospel in spite of persecution?

14 knowing that He who raised the Lord Jesus will raise us also with Jesus and will present us with you.

• In the midst of suffering, what did Paul keep his mind focused on?

15 For all things are for your sakes, so that the grace which is spreading to more and more people may cause the giving of thanks to abound to the glory of God.

16 Therefore we do not lose heart, but though our outer man is decaying, yet our inner man is being renewed day by day.

17 For momentary, light affliction is producing for us an eternal weight of glory far beyond all comparison,

18 while we look not at the things which are seen, but at the things which are not seen; for the things which are seen are temporal, but the things which are not seen are eternal.

• According to verse 17, what is "momentary, light affliction" preparing us for?

• James 1:12 says, "Blessed is a man who perseveres under trial; for once he has been approved, he will receive the crown of life which the Lord has promised to those who love Him." How does this verse help explain Paul's perspective in 2 Corinthians 4:17–18?

WRAP IT UP

Paul described his suffering in 2 Corinthians 1:8 as an excessive burden that was beyond his strength, but in 2 Corinthians 4:17 he described those same sufferings as "momentary, light affliction" that was preparing him for "an eternal weight of glory far beyond all comparison."

Holding this eternal perspective compelled Paul to continue to go out and preach the gospel to all who would hear, knowing the more he preached the more he would suffer. He wrote in 2 Corinthians 4:10–11 of "carrying about in the body the dying of Jesus," of "being delivered over to death for Jesus' sake"—all for the sake of others, that the grace of God would be spread to more and more people, ultimately bringing even greater glory to God.

What about you? When you experience suffering and persecution for the gospel, do you have an eternal perspective? Do you get fired up knowing that this momentary, light affliction is nothing compared to the promise of spending eternity in the presence of God?

Beloved, through this study you have learned that God wants all of your heart, He wants you to love His Word, He wants to answer your prayers, He wants you to give Him the glory due His name. When we do these things, our hearts are stirred and we cannot help but tell others about the wonderful works of the One who took us from death to life. This is why we do not lose heart, this is what fuels our passion: we know the grace we have received from God and we know that others desperately need to hear the good news of the gospel.

Jesus clearly tells us the more we love Him the more we will be hated, but remember the eternal perspective and what our suffering is preparing us for: eternity with Jesus Christ.

> Now to Him who is able to keep you from stumbling, and to make you stand in the presence of His glory blameless with great joy, to the only God our Savior, through Jesus Christ our Lord, be glory, majesty, dominion and authority, before all time and now and forever. Amen. (Jude 24–25)

ABOUT KAY ARTHUR AND PRECEPT MINISTRIES INTERNATIONAL

KAY ARTHUR is known around the world as an international Bible teacher, author, conference speaker, and host of the national radio and television programs *Precepts for Life,* which reach a worldwide viewing audience of over ninety-four million. Recipient of the NRB Hall of Fame Award in 2011, Kay is a four-time Gold Medallion Award–winning author of more than one hundred books and Bible studies. She received an honorary doctorate from Tennessee Temple University.

Kay and her husband, Jack, founded Precept Ministries International in 1970 in Chattanooga, Tennessee, with a vision to establish people in God's Word. Today, the ministry has a worldwide outreach. In addition to inductive-study training workshops and thousands of small-group studies across America, PMI ministers in 180 countries with inductive Bible studies translated into more than seventy languages, discipling people by teaching them how to discover Truth for themselves.

ABOUT MARK SHELDRAKE

MARK SHELDRAKE serves as national director of the Precept Ministries International program in Canada. He has a passion to see God's people established in God's Word.

Prior to coming on staff with Precept in 2007, Mark served the local church for more than fifteen years as a youth pastor and senior pastor and was involved in developing high school impact programs. Mark graduated from Emmanuel Bible College with a bachelor's degree in professional studies with a focus on education and youth. Mark and his wife, Jessica, travel across Canada and internationally, teaching Precept Bible Studies and sharing the gospel.

Contact Precept Ministries International for more information about inductive Bible studies in your area.

Precept Ministries International
PO Box 182218
Chattanooga, TN 37422-7218
800-763-8280
www.precept.org